Should Scientists Pursue Cloning?

Isabel Thomas

Raintree

Chicago, Illinois

www.capstonepub.com
Visit our website to find out more information about Heinemann-Raintree books.

To order:
☎ Phone 888-454-2279
▭ Visit www.capstonepub.com
to browse our catalog and order online.

Edited by Adam Miller, Andrew Farrow, and
 Adrian Vigliano
Designed by Philippa Jenkins
Original illustrations © Capstone Global Library
 Limited 2012
Illustrated by Art Construction p10
Picture research by Mica Brancic
Originated by Capstone Global Library Ltd.
Printed and bound in China by CTPS Ltd.

15 14 13 12 11
10 9 8 7 6 5 4 3 2 1

Library of Congress Cataloging-in-Publication Data
Cataloging-in-Publication Data is on file at the Library of Congress.

ISBNs: 978-1-4109-4463-4 (HC) 978-1-4109-4470-2 (PB)

Acknowledgments
The author and publishers are grateful to the following for permission to reproduce copyright material: Alamy pp. 7 (© Tom Bean), 37 (© Interfoto), 41 (© Kolvenbach); Corbis pp. 4 (Reuters/© Jo Yong-Hak), 5 (© Hulton-Deutsch Collection), 6 (Visuals Unlimited/© Dr. Richard Kessel & Dr. Gene Shih), 13 (© Colin McPherson), 19 (JAI/© Max Milligan), 20 (Reuters/Handout/© Genetic Savings & Clone, Inc.), 21 (Photo courtesy of the College of Veterinary Medicine, Texas A&M University.), 24 (© John Carnemolla), 33 (© Hulton-Deutsch Collection), 38 (Reuters/Choi Byung-gil/© Yonhap), 11 bottom (© Robert Recker); Getty Images pp. 16 (Roll Call/Bill Clark), 32 (AFP Photo/Eric Feferberg), 35 (Mark Mainz); Reuters p. 39 (© Ho New); Rex Features p. 36 (TM & copyright 20th Century Fox./ c.20thC.Fox/Everett); Science Photo Library pp. 11 top (US National Library Of Medicine), 25 (James King-Holmes), 26 (Philippe Psaila), 27 (Klaus Guldbrandsen), 29 (Juergen Berger), 31; Shutterstock pp. 8 (© Todd Boland), 9 (© Nolie), 15 (© Ciapix), 22 (© Anan Kaewkhammul), 23 (© Jason Prince), contents page bottom (© Anan Kaewkhammul), contents page top (© Todd Boland). All background design feature pictures courtesy of Shutterstock.

Main cover photograph of two cloned Turkish Angola cats reproduced with permission of Corbis (Reuters/Choi Byung-gil/Yonhap); inset cover photograph of genetically engineered rice fish reproduced with permission of Reuters (Richard Chung).

The publisher would like to thank literary consultant Nancy Harris and content consultant Ann Fullick for their assistance in the preparation of this book.

Every effort has been made to contact copyright holders of material reproduced in this book. Any omissions will be rectified in subsequent printings if notice is given to the publisher.

Disclaimer
All the Internet addresses (URLs) given in this book were valid at the time of going to press. However, due to the dynamic nature of the Internet, some addresses may have changed, or sites may have changed or ceased to exist since publication. While the author and publisher regret any inconvenience this may cause readers, no responsibility for any such changes can be accepted by either the author or the publisher.

Contents

How do you grow your own clone?

Find out on page 9!

Why is Noah the gaur so important?

Turn to page 22 to find out!

Some words are shown in bold, **like this**. These words are explained in the glossary. You will find important information and definitions underlined, <u>like this</u>.

WHAT IS CLONING?

When many people hear the word "cloning," they imagine identical copies of humans or animals. Science fiction and media stories often make cloning sound bad or scary.

To scientists, cloning has many different meanings. It describes scientific techniques used to find out how living things grow. It is a tool for studying diseases and creating new medicines. It describes processes that have been used by crop farmers for hundreds of years. Researchers are even using cloning to save **endangered species** of plants and animals.

The media likes to report some types of cloning more than others. Pet cloning may make individual owners happy, but some people argue that it is a waste of money.

What is a clone?

A clone is an exact copy of a living thing. This could be a single cell, or sometimes a whole plant or animal. Most results of cloning are smaller than the period at the end of this sentence.

Some cloning techniques used by scientists are controversial, such as cloning farm animals. Scientists, politicians, and the public have to consider the advantages and disadvantages of cloning. They can then decide if the goals of cloning research, such as curing diseases and improving agriculture, make the science worth pursuing.

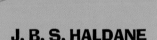

J. B. S. HALDANE

The word "clone" comes from the Greek word *klon*, meaning "twig." Farmers and gardeners have been making copies of plants by cutting off twigs and growing them into new plants for more than 4,000 years. The famous biologist J. B. S. Haldane (1892-1964) was the first person to link the word with the controversial idea of creating identical copies of humans. Haldane studied **genetics** (the study of **genes**), and made accurate predictions about future scientific methods. Genes contain the information living things need to grow. Haldane suggested that in the future, people with extraordinary talents might be cloned.

CLONING IN NATURE

Cloning happens all the time in nature. Your body is made up of **cells**, the smallest parts of any living thing, which are busy making copies of themselves. Some plants and animals clone themselves to produce offspring, a new generation of living things.

There are about 100 trillion cells in your body. Some of your cells can clone themselves to replace old or damaged cells. New cells are also needed for your body to grow. Some types of cells clone themselves more often than others. Millions of new hair, skin, and fingernail cells are created every second.

parent cell

identical new cell

Most cells are very small, and can only be seen with a microscope. This cell is cloning itself to make a new cell. Each new cell gets a copy of the same genetic information.

© Dr. Richard Kessel & Dr. Gene Shih

CLONING A WHOLE ORGANISM

Many plants can **reproduce** (create new individuals) by cloning themselves. Potato plants can do this. Each potato that grows has the potential to grow into a new plant. The new plants have exactly the same genetic information as the parent plant. They are **clones**.

A few animals, including starfish, can also clone themselves to produce offspring. However, most animals and plants reproduce by **sexual reproduction**. This is a process that combines genetic information from two parents. Sexual reproduction mixes up **genetic information** to create plants or animals with different characteristics than their parents. The offspring are not an exact copy of either parent. This natural **variation** (genetic difference) is important. It might create offspring that are better at surviving than their parents.

These aspen trees are clones. They all grew from the same 80,000-year-old root system.

Genetic information

Cloned cells share the same genetic information. This is a set of instructions that tells every cell in your body how to grow and function. Individual instructions are known as genes. Almost every person has a unique set of genes.

7

ARTIFICIAL CLONING

When farmers find an animal that grows well or a plant that tastes great, they want to recreate these characteristics. Farmers have done this for centuries using **selective breeding**. This means they only let the very best animals and plants **reproduce**. However, there is no guarantee that the best pieces of **genetic information** will be passed on to the **offspring**. This is because **sexual reproduction** mixes **genes**. The only way to do this is to make an exact copy, or artificial **clone**, of the animal or plant.

Gardeners and farmers have been artificially **cloning** plants for thousands of years. It allows a plant with useful characteristics to be reproduced cheaply on a huge scale. Two cloning methods are used:

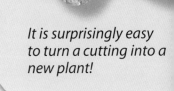

It is surprisingly easy to turn a cutting into a new plant!

- **Taking cuttings**
  The simplest way to clone a plant is to cut a piece off and give the **cutting** the light, water, and nutrients it needs to grow into a new plant. This is so easy that you can do it in your kitchen (see box at right). The new plants have genes that are identical to those of the parent plant.

- **Tissue culture**
  Only a certain number of cuttings can be taken from a plant without killing it. **Tissue culture** works in a similar way, but uses much smaller pieces of the parent plant. A tissue culture uses parent plant **cells** to clone many new plants. This means hundreds or thousands of clones can be created from one plant. Tissue culture is used to mass-produce plants for farming. It is much faster than growing plants from seeds.

...of the things you eat,
...nd wear are made
...cloned plants. All the
...n this apple orchard
...ones of one parent
...he farmer can be sure
...he fruit on every tree
...pen at the same time.

GROW YOUR OWN CLONE

Try cloning a plant by taking a cutting.
To start you will need:
- a parent plant (try basil, begonia, geranium, ivy, or tomato)
- a clean plastic bottle
- a plastic bag

1. Use clean scissors to cut a stem from the parent plant.

2. Remove any leaves from the bottom half of the stem.

3. Fill a plastic bottle with tap water almost to the top. Rest the cutting on the rim of the bottle so that the stem dangles in the water.

4. Place a plastic bag loosely over the bottle, and put the bottle on a sunny windowsill.

5. Change the water every two days, to keep it clean. Watch the stem carefully. Roots will start to sprout from the cut stem in two to four weeks.

6. When the roots are a few inches long, gently plant the stem in a flowerpot filled with potting soil. Add water, and keep the pot on the sunny windowsill. Your clone will soon grow into a full-sized plant.

CLONING ANIMALS

More recently, scientists have found ways to clone animals that normally need two parents to reproduce. <u>Cloning animals is much harder than cloning plants.</u> Farmers can't put an ear or tail cutting from their best cow on a sunny windowsill and wait for it to grow into a calf. However, scientists can split animal cells up at a much earlier stage, when they are **embryos**. Embryos are tiny bundles of cells that keep dividing.

First, they need an embryo. This can be removed from a pregnant animal. Or an egg can be **fertilized** in the lab so it starts to develop into an embryo. This is called **in vitro fertilization (IVF)**. When an embryo is just a few days old, all of its cells are identical. If the embryo is split into two or more pieces, each one can develop into a new individual.

*Offspring created by **embryo splitting** are identical to each other. All their cells share the same genetic information. This information comes from the original mother and father, who are chosen because they have useful qualities.*

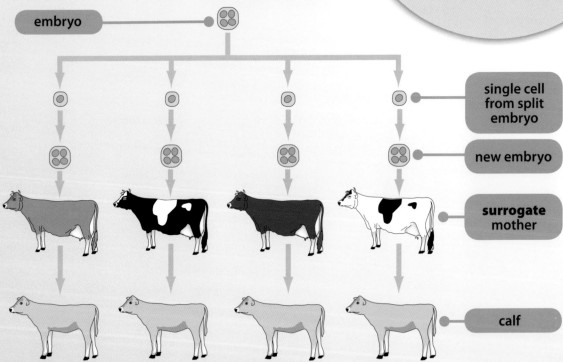

father

mother

embryo

single cell from split embryo

new embryo

surrogate mother

calf

HANS SPEMANN

Many of the methods used to clone animals were discovered as scientists researched other information. German zoologist Hans Spemann (1869-1941) was interested in what makes an embryo develop into different parts of an animal's body. He worked with salamander eggs, which grow into tadpoles outside their mother's body. In 1902, Spemann used a tiny loop of his baby's hair to split a salamander embryo in half. He observed that the two halves grew into two different tadpoles.

SURROGATE MOTHERS

The embryos are put into the **wombs** of surrogate mothers. The womb is the organ where offspring develop before birth. A surrogate is a female that will carry the developing embryo and give birth to the baby animal. Using female animals as surrogate mothers is controversial. Several groups, including animal rights groups, believe that it damages the health of the animals used, and may cause suffering. For example, surrogate mothers of clones are more likely to have difficulty giving birth.

IDENTICAL TWINS

In many animals, including humans, an embryo sometimes splits in half naturally in the womb. Each half develops into a baby. These identical twins share the same genetic information, so they are natural clones. Around 1 in 250 of the women that give birth each year have identical twins.

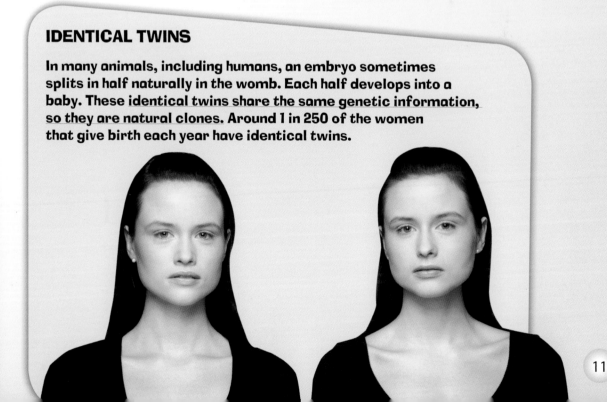

CLONING AN ADULT ANIMAL

The offspring produced by embryo splitting are identical to each other. They are not identical to the mother and father. This means there is no guarantee that the best characteristics of each parent have been passed on. The only way to do this is to clone an adult animal. Scientists can do this using a process called **somatic cell nuclear transfer (SCNT)**. A body cell from an adult animal is "reprogrammed" or adjusted so it becomes an embryo. The baby animal that develops from the embryo has the same genetic information as the animal whose body cell was used. <u>SCNT is what most news reports mean when they say "cloning."</u>

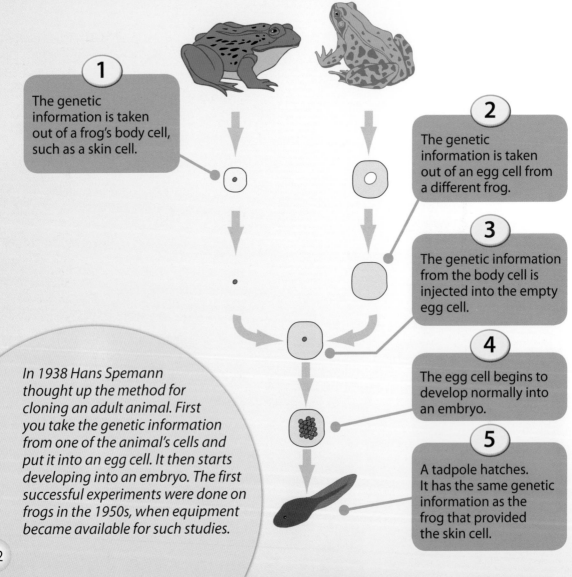

1
The genetic information is taken out of a frog's body cell, such as a skin cell.

2
The genetic information is taken out of an egg cell from a different frog.

3
The genetic information from the body cell is injected into the empty egg cell.

4
The egg cell begins to develop normally into an embryo.

5
A tadpole hatches. It has the same genetic information as the frog that provided the skin cell.

In 1938 Hans Spemann thought up the method for cloning an adult animal. First you take the genetic information from one of the animal's cells and put it into an egg cell. It then starts developing into an embryo. The first successful experiments were done on frogs in the 1950s, when equipment became available for such studies.

THE RACE TO CLONE A MAMMAL

After early experiments with frogs, scientists tried to clone other types of animals, including **mammals**. This was much more difficult. Unlike frogs, mammals don't develop outside their mother's body. Once an embryo was created, it had to be placed into the womb of a surrogate mother.

THE WORLD'S MOST FAMOUS SHEEP

A breakthrough came in 1996, with the birth of Dolly the sheep. Dolly was created using a cell from a six-year-old sheep. A different sheep was the surrogate mother. Dolly was the first mammal to be cloned from an adult "parent," and her birth was reported all around the world. <u>Like many scientific achievements, it was not an overnight success but the result of many years of research.</u> There were 276 failed attempts, which show the difficulty of SCNT.

The birth of Dolly the sheep caused feelings of both wonder and fear.

FROM FARMING TO PHARMING

Some people worried that the scientists who created Dolly the sheep were interfering with nature. The scientists argued that their **cloning** work had an important purpose. They were learning how to make copies of animals with useful qualities.

High quality crops and livestock (farm animals) are very valuable to farmers. **Selective breeding** has been used for centuries to pass on the **genes** of the best plants and animals to the next generation. Selective breeding means only allowing the best animals or plants to **reproduce**. Success is not guaranteed, because **sexual reproduction** mixes the genes of two parents. This creates **variation** or differences.

Cloning produces identical copies of an existing plant or animal. It can be used to ensure that the genes from wheat that grows particularly fast, or a cow that produces a lot of milk, are passed on to **offspring**.

Have I eaten cloned meat or milk?

This is very unlikely. Cloning is still too difficult and expensive to be used routinely. Instead, exceptional cows are cloned and sold to other farmers. They are not used to produce meat and milk, but for breeding high quality offspring that farmers hope will have the best genes from the original animal. Several clones can produce more offspring than one individual.

In the United States, companies are cloning animals that give high yields of meat and milk. Around one thousand of the United States' one million cattle are clones. Milk and meat from the offspring of these cloned animals have entered the food chain in the United States and United Kingdom.

FEEDING THE WORLD

The ultimate goal of cloning livestock is to produce more food for less money. This is why many scientists believe that cloning could help to meet the challenge of feeding the world's growing population. By 2050, it is estimated that our planet will have to support 2.2 billion more people than it has now.

IS CLONED MEAT SAFE?

Scientists have shown that meat and milk from cloned animals and their offspring is safe. In fact, it is impossible to tell the difference between cloned and naturally produced food. Despite this, attitudes to cloned food vary around the world. Some people dislike the idea of eating cloned meat, because it is not created naturally. Others feel that cloning has not been around for long enough to judge the long-term effects on human or animal health.

These protestors don't like the idea of eating meat from cloned animals and are voicing their opposition.

Many people think that it is wrong to clone animals in order to feed humans, because the animals may suffer. Cloning causes health problems in **surrogate** mothers (see page 11) and in the cloned offspring. Many **miscarriages** (pregnancies that end too early) and **stillbirths** (when the baby is not born alive) are reported for every animal that is successfully born. Even successful clones can have **birth defects** that cause them to die at a young age. Cloned animals are often much larger than normal, and have problems with their liver and joints. They also have problems fighting diseases.

HEADLINE NEWS

Science can become very controversial when the public feels that new technologies are being introduced too soon. In 2010, cloning got bad press when it was found that the offspring of a cloned cow had entered the United Kingdom food chain without the proper approval required by law. **Embryos** of a cloned cow living in the United States were brought to the United Kingdom, where two of the calves that developed from the embryos were sold for meat. People argued that they have a right to choose whether or not to buy meat and milk from the offspring of cloned animals. However, the huge scale of farming means it would be very difficult to trace every individual animal and label all foods. Many people believe these problems mean that the cloning of farm animals should be stopped completely.

WHAT IS PHARMING?

Cloning technology can be used to create and replicate (make copies of) **genetically modified (GM)** animals. These are animals that have been given useful genes from other **species**, or types of animals. The technology is quite new, but scientists think it could have many benefits. For example, animals can be given certain human genes so they produce important substances in their milk, blood, or urine. These substances could be extracted and used as medicines for humans. This is the idea behind **pharming**—and it's already happening.

From goat to pharmacy

Antithrombin is a substance needed by patients with a rare but deadly blood condition. Antithrombin extracted from the milk of GM goats was approved in 2006 in the European Union and 2009 in the United States. Before these goats were created, antithrombin had to be extracted from human blood donations. Just one goat produces as much antithrombin in a year as 90,000 blood donations. If more antithrombin is needed, more goats can be bred.

HOW CLONING HELPS

Cloning techniques are used to create the GM animals used in pharming. Cloning also helps scientists to turn one GM animal into a herd that can produce medicine in large quantities. Some companies believe that pursuing this type of cloning research will make it faster, cheaper, safer, and simpler to produce many important medicines.

Pharming is controversial because of worries about the well-being and safety of animals. People are also concerned that medicine-producing animals might enter the food chain by mistake. They also worry that scientists are interfering with nature by creating animals with human genes. Doctors and scientists argue that pharming will be very carefully controlled, and will reduce human suffering.

Pharming can turn a cow into a medicine supply. In the future, cows could be an important source of medicines for poor and remote communities.

BACK FROM THE DEAD

A handful of pets and endangered animals have been cloned, and scientists think the technology could eventually be used to bring **extinct** animals, which no longer exist, "back to life." This sounds like good news, but it also raises some important questions about **cloning**.

High-quality cows and sheep can make farmers a lot of money, but other animals are valuable in different ways. Many pet owners see their cat or dog as a family member, and are devastated when it dies. Several companies around the world now offer to clone pets. This is very expensive, so some pet owners are storing some of their pets' **cells** for the future, when cloning might be cheaper and more reliable.

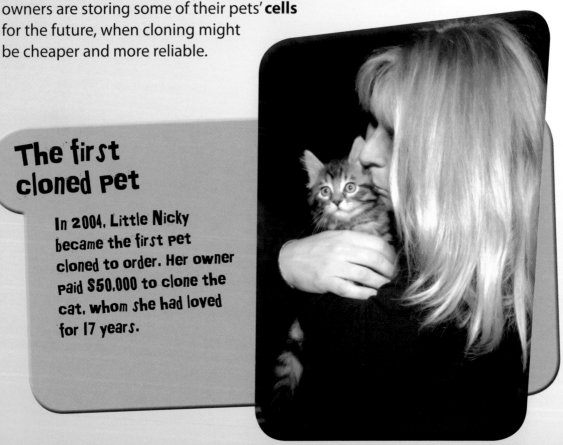

The first cloned pet

In 2004, Little Nicky became the first pet cloned to order. Her owner paid $50,000 to clone the cat, whom she had loved for 17 years.

Two animals can have identical genes, but different colors and markings on their fur. This cloned cat has different markings than the cat she was cloned from.

THE PROBLEMS WITH CLONING PETS

A cloned pet shares the same **genes** as its donor. However, genes don't determine everything about an individual. The environment a pet grows up in influences many of the characteristics that make it unique. One of the most important is personality. Horse owners may want to clone their favourite horse because it is reliable and gentle. But if the **clone** is frightened by a loud noise, it could grow up to be timid and skittish.

A cloned pet may not even look like its donor. The world's first cloned cat, CC, was a copy of a tortoiseshell cat named Rainbow. Although they shared exactly the same genes, CC's fur markings were very different from Rainbow's markings.

Is it fair for cloning companies to take thousands of dollars from people who might not realize that a clone may not look or behave like their beloved original pet?

SAVING ENDANGERED SPECIES

Climate change, population growth, and other human activities threaten to wipe out a million types of plants and animals by 2050. Could cloning boost the numbers of **endangered species** and save them from **extinction**?

Several endangered animals have been cloned already (see box on Noah the gaur). However, cloning an endangered animal is much more difficult than cloning a cow or a sheep. Scientists do not know as much about the bodies of endangered animals. They cannot be taken out of their natural **habitats**, or homes, and studied in labs. Another problem is that hundreds of eggs and several **surrogate** mothers may be needed to produce just one cloned animal. One way to get around this is to use eggs and surrogate mothers from a different **species** that is closely related to the endangered one.

NOAH THE GAUR

Noah the baby gaur was created in 2001, using a frozen skin cell from an adult gaur that had died eight years earlier. The genetic information from the skin cell was put inside an empty egg cell from a normal cow, and a second cow was used as the surrogate mother.

The first endangered animal to be cloned was a gaur, which is a type of wild cow.

Another approach is to focus on endangered animals that are easier to clone. Frogs and toads do not get as much attention as rhinos or tigers, but one in every three species is threatened with extinction. Scientists have known how to successfully clone frogs for over half a century (see page 12).

Some endangered animals that have been cloned

- Gaur (a type of wild cow)
- European mouflon (a type of wild sheep)
- Asian banteng (a type of wild cow)
- Gray wolves

CONSERVATION CONTROVERSY

Some people think that cloning is a good last resort. They say that it is better to keep a species alive by cloning than to completely lose an animal. However, other people are opposed to cloning. They worry that the public will think these animals don't need to be protected anymore. They would rather have the money and effort that goes into cloning research put toward protecting animals and their natural habitats.

FIGHTING EXTINCTION

The birth of Noah the gaur was exciting because it showed that clones can be created from frozen cells. Could the same be done with cells from frozen woolly mammoths found in Siberia, or other extinct animals?

Scientists in Australia have been trying to clone the extinct Tasmanian tiger for more than 12 years. The last Tasmanian tiger died around 70 years ago. The scientists are using cells from a small Tasmanian tiger puppy that was preserved in alcohol in 1866. Other scientists believe it would be better to devote the time and money to saving Australia's living endangered animals.

Cloning extinct animals such as the Tasmanian tiger (shown above) will be very difficult, and success is likely to be a long way in the future.

Special projects store plant seeds and animal cells to protect against extinction.

Pyrenean ibex

In 2009, scientists managed to clone an extinct mountain goat called the Pyrenean ibex. Of the 439 cloned embryos that were made, only 57 were healthy enough to put into surrogate mothers. Seven of these surrogates became pregnant and just one live Pyrenean ibex was born.

GENE BANKS

Conservation scientists are collecting and freezing cells from endangered species to protect against future animal extinction. Projects like the San Diego, California, Frozen Zoo and the United Kingdom's Frozen Ark store cells from thousands of animals that are likely to go extinct in the next 50 years. The cells are stored in a very cold liquid where they should be able to survive for hundreds or even thousands of years. Scientists of the future might be able to use improved cloning technology to bring these possibly extinct animals back from the dead.

CLONING HUMAN CELLS

When Dolly the sheep was cloned from an adult **mammal**, it was reported around the world. Many reports said that the next step would be **cloning** humans, because we are mammals, too.

However, most scientists are not interested in trying to clone whole humans. Many have said that trying to do this would be **unethical**, which means wrong according to scientific ideas (see page 30). However, many researchers are cloning human **cells** to find new ways to fight disease.

CURING CANCER BY CLONING CELLS

In 2008, a team of U.S. scientists reported that they had treated skin cancer by cloning a patient's own immune cells (white blood cells that help the body to attack disease) and putting them back into his body. The army of billions of white blood cells destroyed the patient's tumors (growths caused by cancer). This research is in the very early stages, but using a patient's own cells avoids the dangerous side effects of other cancer treatments.

This researcher is choosing an egg cell to use for cloning a cow.

STEM CELL THERAPY

Another type of human cell that scientists are very interested in cloning is a **stem cell**. Stem cells are "master cells" that can develop into other types of body cells. For example, blood stem cells in your **bone marrow** (soft inside part of some bones) make important new blood cells throughout your life. If these stem cells are taken out of a healthy person and injected into a patient, they can produce enough blood cells to treat certain diseases. This is known as stem cell therapy.

Special stem cells are found inside very young **embryos**. They are special because stem cells from embryos can grow into any type of body cell (such as an organ cell). Scientists hope that one day they will be able to use these cells to treat thousands of serious diseases. For example, new heart cells could replace muscle damaged by heart disease.

HOW IS CLONING LINKED TO STEM CELLS?

If donated stem cells are not an exact match, a patient's body will attack and reject them. The cloning technology used to create Dolly offers a solution. One of a patient's body cells, such as a skin cell, could be turned into an embryo. The stem cells inside this embryo, and any body cells grown from them, would be an exact match to the patient. This is called **therapeutic cloning**.

Therapeutic cloning is a very new science and has not produced any treatments yet. If it works, it will give doctors the power to change one human cell to produce any other type of cell or tissue the donor needs.

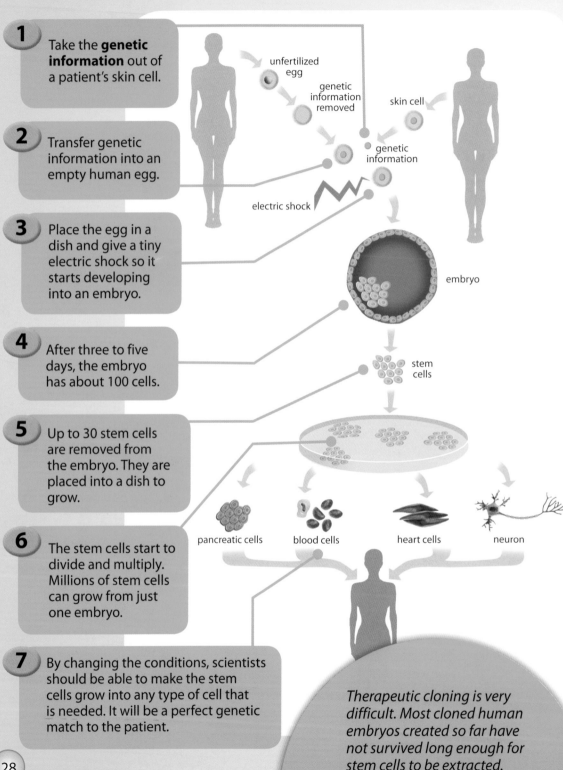

1 Take the **genetic information** out of a patient's skin cell.

2 Transfer genetic information into an empty human egg.

3 Place the egg in a dish and give a tiny electric shock so it starts developing into an embryo.

4 After three to five days, the embryo has about 100 cells.

5 Up to 30 stem cells are removed from the embryo. They are placed into a dish to grow.

6 The stem cells start to divide and multiply. Millions of stem cells can grow from just one embryo.

7 By changing the conditions, scientists should be able to make the stem cells grow into any type of cell that is needed. It will be a perfect genetic match to the patient.

unfertilized egg

genetic information removed

skin cell

genetic information

electric shock

embryo

stem cells

pancreatic cells   blood cells   heart cells   neuron

Therapeutic cloning is very difficult. Most cloned human embryos created so far have not survived long enough for stem cells to be extracted.

There are two main uses for therapeutic cloning:

1 Creating replacement human cells or even whole organs (body parts) for patients who need them. <u>Stem cells from cloned embryos would be an exact match to the patient, and there would be no need to wait for someone to donate an organ.</u> In the United States, 18 people waiting for a donated organ die every day.

2 Using stem cells from cloned embryos to learn more about diseases and develop new medicines. <u>By creating stem cells from people with specific diseases, scientists can find out more about how the diseases develop.</u> Scientists could also test new medicines on tissues grown from the stem cells. This could mean an end to animal testing.

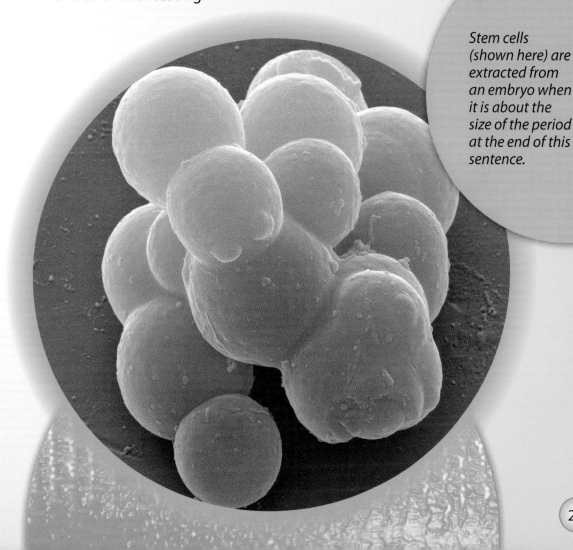

Stem cells (shown here) are extracted from an embryo when it is about the size of the period at the end of this sentence.

IS THERAPEUTIC CLONING ETHICAL?

Creating cloned human embryos for stem cell research is controversial. It is strictly controlled in many countries and banned in some. However, many people argue that scientists should be allowed to pursue this type of cloning because it has the potential to save and improve lives.

The organizations that regulate scientific research consider arguments for and against **therapeutic cloning**. They have to weigh the impact of new developments on individuals and society as a whole. Finding cures for diseases such as heart disease and cancer could benefit millions of people in the future. However, people opposed to therapeutic cloning argue that this is unfair to individuals involved in the research.

INDIVIDUAL EMBRYOS

Stem cells are extracted when an embryo is five days old. Doing this destroys the embryo. Many groups argue that every embryo has the potential to become a human and has the same right to life that we have. They believe it is **unethical** to create a human life only to destroy it. Others say that five-day-old embryos are not yet humans, because they are tiny balls of **cells** without thoughts or feelings.

WHO ELSE MIGHT BE HARMED?

A large supply of unfertilized human eggs is needed to create cloned stem cells. Eggs can be taken from a woman's body. But this involves taking high levels of certain drugs. Some doctors believe this may put women's health at risk. Some people worry that women living in poverty would be tempted to undergo this procedure to earn money.

FROM CONTROVERSY TO CURES

Many everyday medical procedures were once controversial. For many centuries, experiments on human bodies were banned or frowned upon, and done in secret. However, the experiments carried out by scientists helped doctors understand the human body. Supporters of therapeutic cloning argue that it is unethical to block research that could improve health care.

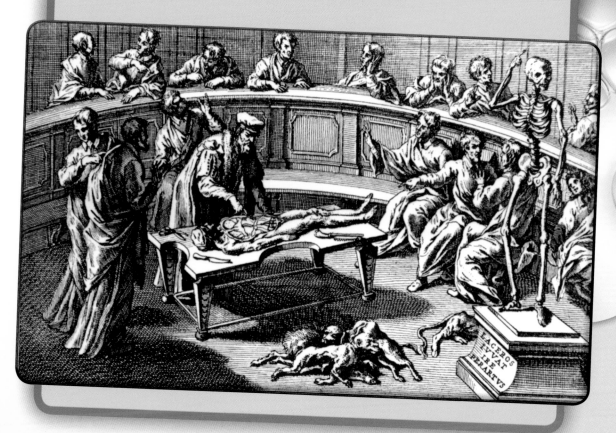

These difficult issues have led to therapeutic cloning research being strictly controlled in many countries. Opponents say that researchers should put effort and money into developing other sources of stem cells. However, groups of patients and many scientists argue that this will delay development of treatments that could save lives.

HUMAN CLONING

The goal of **therapeutic cloning** is to collect **stem cells** that can be used to study and treat diseases. However, some people worry that it will lead to the creation of cloned human beings.

An **embryo** cannot develop into a baby in a laboratory. In order to become a baby, the cloned embryo must be put into the **womb** of a **surrogate** mother. This is the process that has been used to clone many different **species** of **mammals**. This is known as **human reproductive cloning**. It has never been attempted by respected scientists, but people have asked if it could—and should—be pursued.

Replicating people with amazing talents, such as the athlete Usain Bolt, sounds like a good idea. But would it be fair to countries that could not afford to use cloning technology?

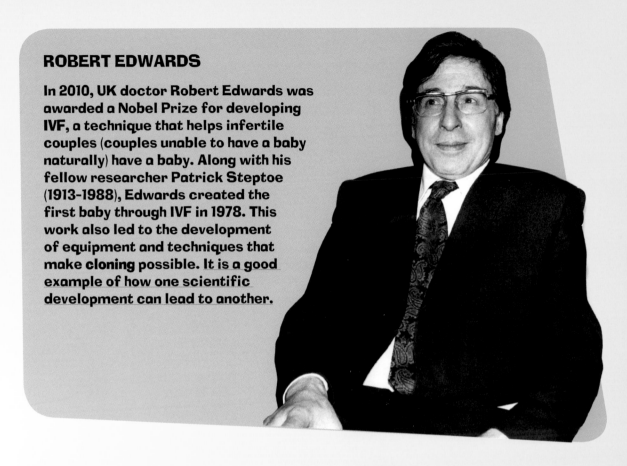

ROBERT EDWARDS

In 2010, UK doctor Robert Edwards was awarded a Nobel Prize for developing IVF, a technique that helps infertile couples (couples unable to have a baby naturally) have a baby. Along with his fellow researcher Patrick Steptoe (1913-1988), Edwards created the first baby through IVF in 1978. This work also led to the development of equipment and techniques that make **cloning** possible. It is a good example of how one scientific development can lead to another.

WHY WOULD ANYONE WANT TO CLONE A HUMAN?

Science is often driven by the need to improve life for individuals or society as a whole. Here are some reasons that might drive research into human reproductive cloning:

1 To bring back a loved one, such as a child who died at a young age.

2 To save a life. Cloning could create an identical twin sibling, or "savior sibling" to donate tissues or organs for transplant.

3 To help an infertile person have a baby, who shares that parent's **genetic information**.

COULD SCIENTISTS CLONE HUMANS?

Even if a scientific development has the potential to help people, the way it is achieved may raise ethical issues. This is the case with human reproductive cloning.

BIOETHICS

Bioethics is a set of guidelines for deciding whether scientific research, such as human cloning, is right or wrong. Ethical decisions are made by weighing the overall impact of an action on the health and well-being of humans.

Fertility techniques (methods) such as IVF were used successfully in animals for many years before they were first applied to humans. Cloning technology is very new. Many **clones** that are born have **birth defects** that cause them to die at a young age. Most people, including scientists, believe that it would be **unethical** to carry out such a risky process using human embryos.

Many governments around the world have looked at the evidence and decided that cloning technologies are not safe enough to use on humans. Human reproductive cloning has been banned in more than 50 countries.

IMPOSSIBLE TASK?

Primates (animals such as monkeys, apes, and lemurs) are our closest living relatives, sharing up to 98.4 percent of our **genes**. Despite many attempts, no one has managed to clone a primate. Some scientists believe it may actually prove impossible to clone humans.

Many science fiction stories have explored ideas about cloning.

Clonaid

A company called Clonaid claims to have cloned several humans since 2002. It has never offered any proof, so most scientists believe the claims are false, and disapprove of them. Harry Griffin, one of the scientists who worked on Dolly the sheep, said that it is "entirely unacceptable for groups like Clonaid to be gambling with the health of children."

Some people fear that cloned humans would be treated badly. This happens in the science fiction book and film Never Let Me Go, *in which clones are created so their organs can be used for transplants.*

SHOULD SCIENTISTS CLONE HUMANS?

Most scientists agree that cloning technology will never be safe enough to use on humans. Even if it were, there are other important arguments against it. These range from ethical concerns about how clones would be treated to moral arguments against interfering with nature. <u>Scientists, individuals, and society need to weigh the advantages and disadvantages of new developments before making decisions.</u>

Some people argue that cloned humans would never be able to lead a normal life. Unlike other humans, they would not have two biological parents. If their genetic donor was an adult, they may spend their lives knowing how they would age and what diseases they might get in the future. A clone created to be a "savior sibling" might feel they had no choice but to do the job they were created for, such as donating a kidney.

What about the rights of potential donors? If clones could be created from a single skin **cell**, there is a risk that someone's genetic identity could be "stolen" and cloned without the donor knowing. The rights of surrogate mothers would also need to be protected. Women on low incomes may be used unfairly as egg donors or surrogate mothers (see page 30).

NATURE VERSUS NURTURE

If a clone was created to replace a child who had died, there is a danger that it would be rejected by the parents if it failed to live up to expectations. <u>A clone is an exact genetic copy of the donor, but genes do not control everything about a person.</u> Like CC the cat (see page 21), even appearance is influenced by random changes as we develop. Our environment plays a huge part in how we grow and develop, influencing everything from our weight and height to our personalities.

(see page 21)

The rights of clones

Human cloning raises many difficult questions. For example, if one of your skin cells was used to create a "new you," would you see yourself as the parent, twin sibling, or owner of the clone? Should the clone have the same rights as you? The United Nations has said that if human reproductive cloning ever did happen, laws should be made to protect the rights of clones, to prevent discrimination (being treated differently).

BRAVE NEW WORLD

Fears about human cloning are the basis of many science fiction books. One of the most famous is *Brave New World*, published by Aldous Huxley in 1932, over half a century before the birth of Dolly the sheep. Huxley imagined a world in which cloned humans were created to be slaves, carrying out jobs that no one else wanted to do.

CLONING AND THE MEDIA

Where do you find out about the latest developments in **cloning** research? It is very unlikely that you will visit a lab where cloning research takes place, talk to a research scientist, or read a scientific journal. <u>Most people learn about scientific developments from the media.</u>

Public views about science, including your views, are important. They influence the decisions of people who make laws governing scientific research. <u>If the media doesn't report scientific developments properly, it can create myths and misunderstandings that harm scientific progress.</u>

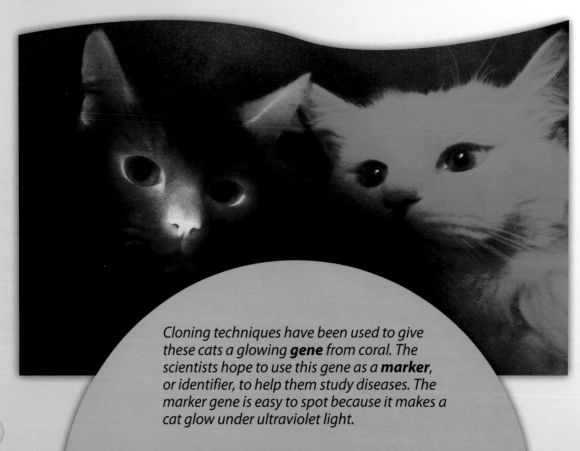

*Cloning techniques have been used to give these cats a glowing **gene** from coral. The scientists hope to use this gene as a **marker**, or identifier, to help them study diseases. The marker gene is easy to spot because it makes a cat glow under ultraviolet light.*

Scientific research is often misrepresented in the media, especially when it involves something as controversial as cloning. Small advances are often reported as breakthroughs that bring human cloning one step closer to reality. However, most cloning research is about exploring **cell** development or disease and has nothing to do with **human reproductive cloning**. Journalists often focus on human cloning because it generates attention-grabbing headlines.

Sometimes "scare" stories fail to explain what the researchers are trying to achieve. A good example is the headline "Cloned Cats Glow Red in the Dark," which appeared in a newspaper in 2007. The story did not explain why the cats were made to glow, which could give the public the impression that the scientists are interfering with nature.

HOW TO ASSESS A SCIENCE STORY

When you read a news report about cloning, check that the research being reported was published first in a trusted scientific journal. This is where scientists present their findings so that they can be tested and replicated by other scientists. Science is sometimes misrepresented by the reporting scientists themselves. Look for comments about the significance of the research from scientists who were not involved in it. Most progress in science is not made as overnight breakthroughs but in small steps over many months or years.

Some news reports reflect the public's fears about cloning. Other stories, such as the one shown here, show a more positive side of the cloning debate.

CONCLUSION

There are many types of **cloning**. Some of them are already widely used by scientists as tools for research. Others may create benefits in the future. These include creating **stem cells** for medicines, helping the world to feed its growing population, or saving endangered animals and plants.

Achieving these goals will involve many more years of research. Some of this research might involve controversial cloning techniques, such as **therapeutic cloning**. Scientists, politicians, and the public must decide if the potential advantages from pursuing cloning research balance the disadvantages. This decision should be based on facts rather than myths and misunderstandings.

SHOULD SCIENTISTS PURSUE CLONING?

Most experts think that an overall yes or no answer to this question would not be good. The best approach is to review each use of cloning on a case-by-case basis. This will involve considering:

- ethical questions (such as, "Are animal rights protected?")
- moral questions (such as, "Is it okay to change nature?")
- and technical questions (such as, "Is the technology good enough to succeed?")

Position of the United Nations

Currently, every country decides its own laws on cloning. Some people argue that an international law is needed. In 2005, the United Nations recommended that all types of human cloning be banned. They have since said that therapeutic cloning could be an exception, but should be carefully controlled by international guidelines.

WHAT ABOUT HUMAN CLONING?

Most scientists and many people who make laws believe that research into stem cells is worth pursuing to help scientists understand and cure diseases. However, reproductive cloning is likely to remain too dangerous for humans. Even if the technical problems are overcome, it is likely to remain controversial.

In 2010, scientists pieced together **genetic information** from Neanderthals, ancient humans that died out around 30,000 years ago. Imagine that cloning technology of the future could bring these ancient humans back to life. Would this be a good idea? This photo shows a Neanderthal model in a museum.

CLONING MYTHS BUSTED!

MYTH:

ONE DAY SCIENTISTS WILL BE ABLE TO CLONE DINOSAURS

Truth: Several science fiction authors have written about how amazing it would be to use **cloning** to bring back animals that became **extinct** millions of years ago. However, it is very unlikely that we'll ever be able to clone dinosaurs by using their bones. Scientists need whole **cells**, rather than the small scraps of **genetic information** found in bones.

MYTH:

CLONING COULD BE USED TO CREATE ARMIES OF CLONES

Truth: It would be impossible to create an army of identical soldiers by cloning one very good soldier. Even though clones have identical **genes**, they would have different **surrogate** mothers and would grow up in different environments. Also, if cloning were ever allowed, there would likely be strict laws to protect the rights of clones (see page 36). They would have the same choices as other humans, and could not be sent into battle against their will.

MYTH:

WOMEN WILL BE ABLE TO HAVE BABIES BY CLONING THEMSELVES, SO THE WORLD WON'T NEED MEN ANYMORE

Truth: If cloning were ever used to help people have children, it would only be as a last resort. It would be too expensive and difficult to be widely used. Also, most humans have a strong desire to have children with the person whom they are in love with, and this has been the case for thousands of years.

MYTH:

YOU COULD CREATE A COPY OF YOURSELF TO TAKE YOUR EXAMS

Truth: Cloning creates an **embryo** that would develop into a baby and then a child at the same speed you did. It would take many years before the clone was the age you are now, by which time you may have finished taking exams for life!

MYTH:

CLONING COULD BE USED TO BRING ALBERT EINSTEIN, MAHATMA GANDHI, OR ADOLF HITLER BACK TO LIFE

Truth: Cloning only passes on genetic information. Genes influence personality, behavior, and achievements but environment also plays a huge part in shaping a person. It would be impossible to recreate the exact environment the donor grew up in, which involves everything from family members to a certain time in history.

MYTH:

SCIENTISTS DON'T NEED TO CREATE CLONED EMBRYOS TO GET STEM CELLS BECAUSE THERE ARE OTHER SOURCES

Truth: Although there are other types of **stem cells**, stem cells from embryos are very special. Many scientists, doctors, and patient groups think we should pursue all types of stem cell research to get new treatments for diseases and conditions as quickly as possible.

Glossary

birth defect physical problem that is present at birth

bone marrow soft tissue found at the center of certain bones

cell smallest parts, or building blocks, of a plant or animal

clone exact copy of something, such as a living thing

cloning process of making a clone

cutting part removed from a plant, which can be used to grow a new plant

embryo tiny bundle of cells, formed in the first few days of a new human or animal life

embryo splitting method of cloning, where a very young embryo is split to make two or more embryos that will develop into offspring that are genetically identical

endangered species group of animals or plants that are in danger of dying out

extinct when a group of animals or plants has died out completely

extinction state of no longer existing

fertilized egg cell that has joined with a sperm cell, giving it the potential to develop into an embryo in the right conditions

gene part of the genetic information of a living thing. Most genes tell cells how to make a particular protein.

genetic information set of instructions that tells every cell of a living thing how to grow and function

genetically modified (GM) plant or animal that has been given one or more genes from a different type of plant or animal, in order to give it useful new qualities

genetics study of genes

habitat natural environment or home of a living thing

human reproductive cloning process of putting a cloned human embryo in the womb of a surrogate mother

in vitro fertilization (IVF) medical technique developed to help infertile people to have a baby. The techniques are also used by scientists in cloning and other research.

mammal warm-blooded animal that makes milk for its young

marker gene that is inserted into the genetic information of a plant or animal, and has an effect that is easy to see. This allows scientists to trace how the gene is passed on from parent to offspring.

miscarriage pregnancy that ends before the fetus is fully grown

offspring new individuals produced when a plant or animal reproduces. Human offspring are called children.

pharming term for giving crops and farm animals certain human genes, using GM technology, so that they produce important human proteins that can be used to make medicines

reproduce create new individuals that share some or all of their genetic information with the parent

selective breeding only allowing the best plants or animals to breed, in order to pass their characteristics on to the next generation

sexual reproduction generate offspring by sexual means

somatic cell nuclear transfer (SCNT) method of cloning an adult animal, by taking the genetic information from one of its cells and placing it in an empty egg cell to create an embryo. This is what most news reports mean when they talk about cloning.

species group of living things that can breed with each other

stem cell type of animal cell that does not have a special job. Instead, a stem cell acts like a cell factory, making one or more types of cell when the animal's body needs them.

stillbirth when a human or animal baby is not born alive

surrogate female who carries a developing fetus, which has been created using an egg cell from a different female

therapeutic cloning matching stem cells to a patient using a cloning process

tissue culture method of cloning plants. A small piece of tissue, or just a few cells, are taken from the parent plant and used to grow hundreds or thousands of new plants.

unethical wrong, according to the principles that scientists and society are working by

variation differences between individuals in a group of plants or animals, caused by small differences in their genetic information

womb female organ where offspring develop before birth

Find Out More

Books

Keyser, Amber. *Decoding Genes with Max Axiom*. Mankato, MN: Capstone Press, 2010.

Maskell, Hazel and Adam Larkum. *What's Biology All About?* London: Usborne Publishing, 2009.

Morgan, Sally. *Body Doubles: Cloning Plants and Animals*. Chicago, IL: Heinemann Library, 2009.

Rooney, Anne. *Medicine: Stem Cells, Genes, and Superbeams*. Chicago, IL: Heinemann Library, 2006.

Winston, Robert. *Evolution Revolution*. New York, NY: DK Publishing, 2009.

Winston, Robert. *What Makes Me, Me?* New York, NY: DK Publishing, 2009.

Websites

www.genome.gov/Glossary
This fantastic talking glossary will tell and show you everything you need to know about genes and genetic research!

http://learn.genetics.utah.edu/content/tech/cloning/
This site provides interactive introductions to cloning. You can even try it yourself in the mouse cloning laboratory.

www.sciencemuseum.org.uk/WhoAmI/FindOutMore/Yourgenes.aspx
This site shows an animated explanation of how and why your genes make you unique.

www.sciencemuseum.org.uk/antenna/dolly/index.asp
Check out this site to explore the history of the world's most famous clone.

Topics to research

Bringing back the Tasmanian tiger

Research the history of the extinct Tasmanian tiger, and the arguments for and against using cloning techniques to bring it back to life. Begin your search here: http://australianmuseum.net.au/The-Thylacine.

Saving the Wollemi pine

Find out how cloning helped Australian conservationists save the Wollemi pine. Start at www.wollemipine.com. Why not find out if there is a Wollemi pine near your school?

Stem cells

Use newspaper and science news websites to search for information on the most recent developments in stem cell research.

Human cloning

Ask a librarian to help you find science fiction inspired by cloning, such as Kazuo Ishiguro's *Never Let Me Go*. If possible, compare several stories. Do they present cloning as a good or a bad thing?

Cloning in nature

Research examples of plants and animals that reproduce by cloning themselves. How many can you find in your kitchen, fridge, or garden? Start by typing "asexual reproduction" into a search engine.

Index